THE TAKE TEN CREW™
AND THE THREE O'CLOCK FIGHT

Written By:
Jaivon Berry
Symone Berry
Patrick Dixon
Devon Hill
Aaliya Hunt
Miranda Jenner
Cecilia Molina
Crystal Olser
Gabrielle Robinson
Scott Smithburn
Kristi Vandervort
Suzanne Vandervort

Lead Story Directors:
Agustin Fuentes, Ph.D. & Andy Kostielney

Ilustrated By:
Doressa Buckingham
Malcolm Fredrick
Brandon Reed
Deshawn Smith
Sara Sullivan
Frank Sullivan
Walter Turner

Lead Art Director & Digital Colorist:
Ian Strandberg

Workshop Artists & Inkers:
John Thompson & Joshua Cuthbert

Lettering & Graphic Artist:
Tim O'Connor
Notre Dame Media Group

Project Coordinator:
Jess Collado

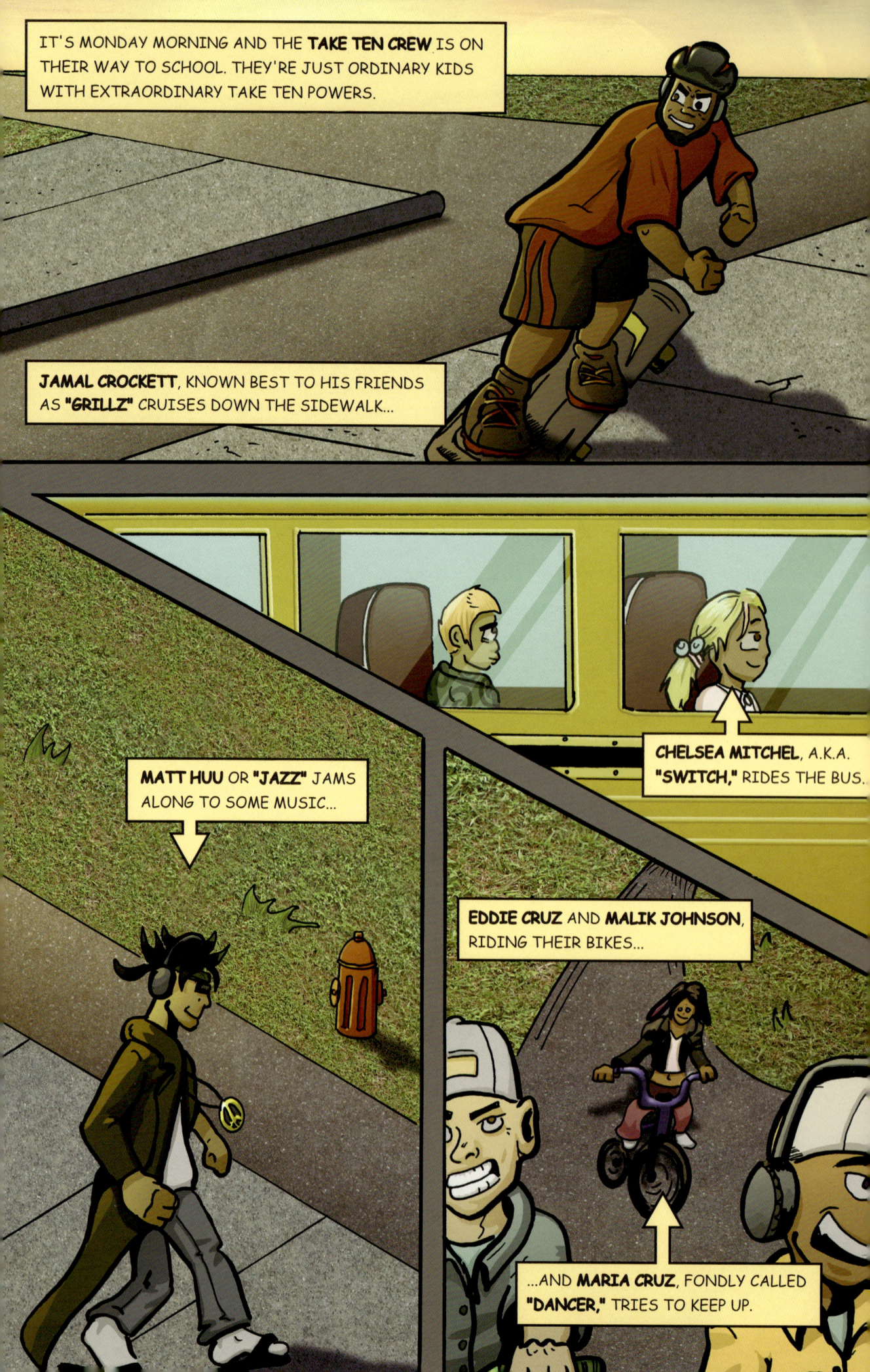

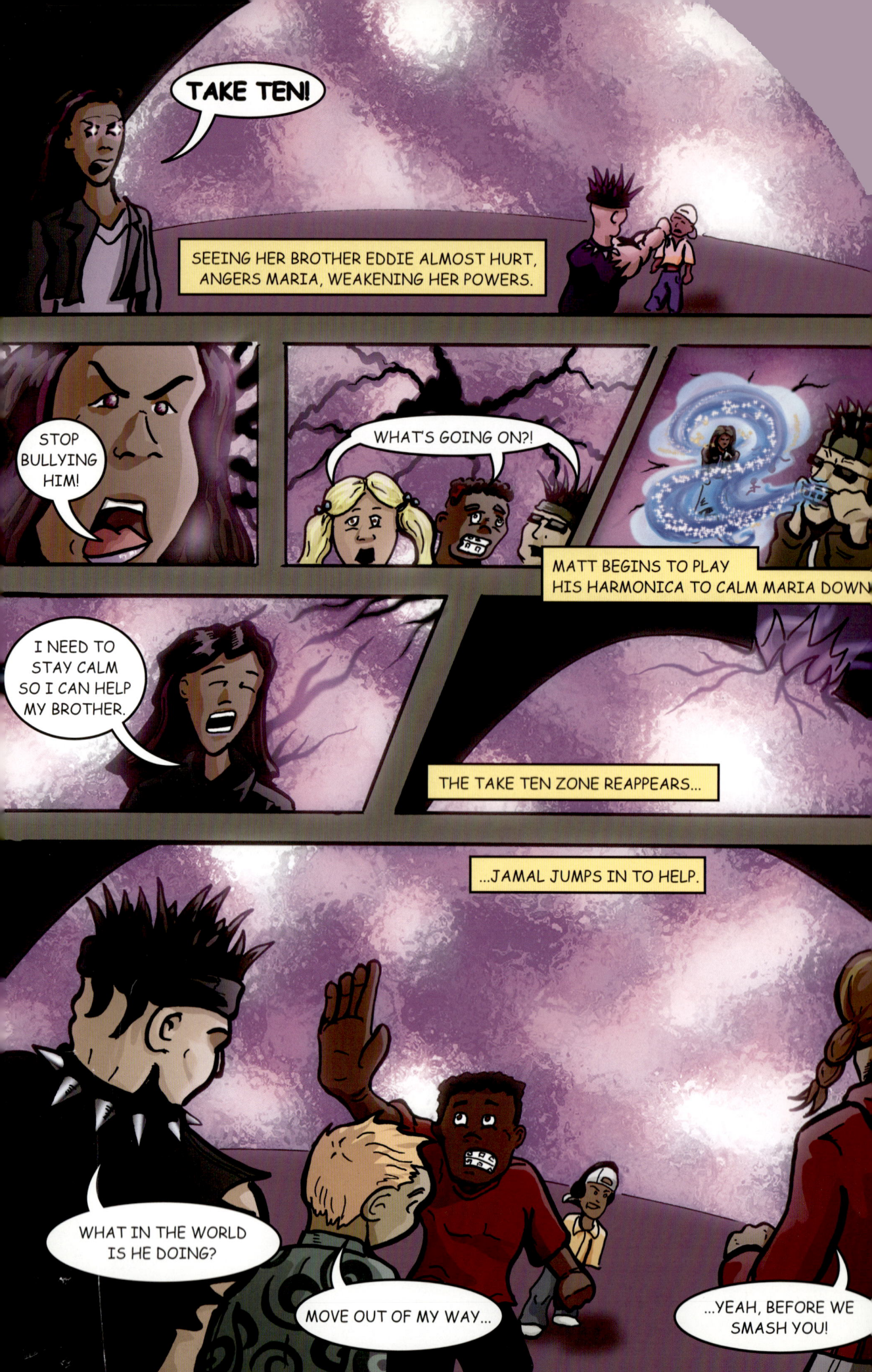

"NOW THAT'S NOT RIGHT! HASN'T THERE BEEN ENOUGH VIOLENCE FOR ONE DAY?"

ON THE WAY HOME FROM SCHOOL, MATT AND JAMAL SEE A GROUP OF KIDS UNDER THE BRIDGE.

MATT AND JAMAL APPROACH THE GANG BUT THEY RUN AWAY.

"LET'S GET OUT OF HERE AND FINISH THIS TOMORROW!"

"THIS IS A PROBLEM FOR ANOTHER DAY."

Take Ten Comic Book Project:
The Making of "The Take Ten Crew™ and the Three O'Clock Fight"

Summary

The Take Ten staff and advisory board members designed the Comic Book project to inspire and encourage young artists and storytellers, funneling their creative energy into a product that would not only uniquely spread a message of non-violence, but also provide a potential source of income for the program. After conducting several focus groups in primary and intermediate centers in the South Bend community, the Take Ten staff chose bullying as the main theme of the comic. Ultimately twenty students had a direct hand in the creation of the book throughout workshops held in July, September and October of 2006.

Summer Workshops

During July 11–13, 2006, Take Ten held workshops for students from local primary and intermediate centers as well as high schools, which focused on the various aspects of developing a comic book. Eleven 3rd–8th graders, who had been Take Ten representatives in their schools during the year, worked for two days with Professor Agustin Fuentes of the Notre Dame Anthropology Department as well as other staff from the Robinson Community Learning Center, to develop the characters, storyline, and dialogue for the comic book. Nine 8th–12th graders began work with local artist Ian Strandberg, as well as Notre Dame art students, on the character sketches and background designs. These students were nominated by the art teachers from their respective schools for both talent and interest in comic books. Before they left the workshops, each was assigned one to two pages of the comic to work on at home.

Saturday Workshops

At the end of the summer, the Take Ten comic book committee reconvened to assess the individual work that the student artists had completed after the workshops. While their work was incredible, it was clear that if the comic book was going to have the consistency and readability the staff and youth had envisioned, it would be necessary to spend greater one-on-one time with each of the student artists. More importantly, the student artists agreed that they needed space to compare their work on a weekly basis so that their characters and backgrounds had similar qualities, while their individual styles remained distinct. Seven of the original nine student artists agreed to come together every Saturday during September and October in order to continue to meet with local artists and Take Ten staff. The artists and staff working with the students witnessed not only an improvement in the student artists' drawing skills but also in their overall behavior and attention spans, and most importantly their ability to communicate ideas to each other. One eighth grader shared, "I could draw at home but I can come here on Saturdays and really do something."

Art Finalization

Although artists Ian Strandberg, Joshua Cuthbert, and John Thompson began to teach the student artists the basics of inking and coloring a comic book, the last steps of the project required a more experienced hand. Both John and Josh inked the pages that the student artists had sketched out, passing them to Ian who digitally colored the entire book. Finally, Tim O'Connor of the Notre Dame Media Group and Ian finished the lettering and sound effects for the book.

Additional Contributions in Production

This project could not have been completed without the support of Mossberg & Co. Inc. A grant from ArtsEverywhere, an initiative of the Community Foundation of St. Joseph County, as well as a matching grant from the University of Notre Dame covered the majority of the additional costs. United Art and Education, Notre Dame Community Relations, The South Bend Regional Museum of Art, Barnaby's Pizza, The State Café and Hot Doggin' provided additional in-kind support.

Final Thanks

We would like to thank all of the sponsors that made this project possible and also all of the youth that had a hand in its creation. It is truly an amazing collaboration and we hope that it provides a useful resource for teachers, parents, and youth across the country.

Gallery of Concept Sketches